Coronavirus and Kids: Comforting Your Child

by Fern Reiss

Peanut Butter and Jelly Press
Boston, Massachusetts

Also by this author:

The Family Guide to Quarantine

The Publishing Game: Find an Agent in 30 Days,
The Publishing Game: Publish a Book in 30 Days, and
The Publishing Game: Bestseller in 30 Days
(all Writer's Digest Book Club selections)

The Infertility Diet: Get Pregnant and Prevent Miscarriage
(an Independent Book Publishers Association
Benjamin Franklin award winner)

Terrorism and Kids: Comforting Your Child
(an American Booksellers Association Booksense 76
winner)

The Breast Cancer Checklist

Fern runs the Expertizing "*Strategize, Publicize,*
Monetize" online course for small businesses at:
```
Courses.Expertizing.com
```

This book is dedicated to everyone on the front lines of the coronavirus pandemic, particularly our medical warriors.

Thank you.

Copyright © 2020 Fern Reiss
Printed in the United States of America.

All rights reserved. No part of this book may be used or reproduced in any manner whatsoever without written permission from the publisher.

For information on quantity discounts to schools and groups, please contact the publisher:

Peanut Butter and Jelly Press
P.O. Box 590239
Newton, MA 02459-0002
(617) 630-0945
info@PeanutButterandJellyPress.com
www.PeanutButterandJellyPress.com

Library of Congress Cataloging-in-Publication Data
Names: Reiss, Fern, author.
Title: Coronavirus and kids : comforting your child / Fern Reiss.
Description: Boston : Peanut Butter and Jelly Press, 2020. | Summary: "Coronavirus and Kids: Comforting Your Child is an invaluable guide for parents and teachers who are faced with children's difficult questions during these difficult times. This book includes dozens of practical tips for minimizing kids' fears without being overprotective, and specific answers to questions children may ask. You'll learn how to talk about coronavirus with your preschoolers, elementary school children, and teenagers, and how to help them feel safe again. By the author of The Family Guide to Quarantine"-- Provided by publisher.
Identifiers: LCCN 2020027067 (print) | LCCN 2020027068 (ebook) | ISBN 9781893290105 (trade paperback) | ISBN 9781893290112 (kindle edition)
Subjects: LCSH: COVID-19 (Disease) | Children--Miscellanea.
Classification: LCC RA644.C67 R45 2020 (print) | LCC RA644.C67 (ebook) | DDC 616.2/414--dc23
LC record available at https://lccn.loc.gov/2020027067
LC ebook record available at https://lccn.loc.gov/2020027068

10 9 8 7 6 5 4 3 2 1

Acknowledgements

I would like to thank the people who helped me work through the weighty and difficult issues in this book, so that it would be accessible to parents and address the very real problems we face in processing these situations with our children.

Thanks to all the psychologists, the doctors, and the stress counselors who shared their thoughts with me over the years. Without your psychological nudges I never could have done it.

Thanks to everyone who helped me rush this book into production, so that it would be available for parents who needed it yesterday.

Thanks to my children, Benjamin, Daniel, and Ariel; and most of all, to my husband, Jonathan, who has become resigned, if not enthusiastic, about my saying, "Just womp it up" about absolutely everything.

Contents

Preface	13
Introduction	15
What about the children?	16
Who is this book for?	17
How is a pandemic different?	18
Will my child be ok?	22
What's inside?	23
Strategies for Helping Your Child	27
Limit television and internet viewing	29
Limit your news viewing	31
Don't let your children listen alone	33
Exhibit your emotions	35
Offer personal reassurance	37
Keep to your routine	39
Talk to your children	41
Talk at your child's level	43
And let them talk to you	45
And let them say what they want	47
Don't lie to your children	49
Convey a sense of hope	51
Be patient	53
Give them options	55

Let them be helpful	57
Enhance their self esteem	59
Make lists	61
Maintain your children's behavior standards	63
Understand sleep patterns may change	65
Be alert for personality changes	67
Watch for anger	69
Listen for complaints of bruises	71
Watch for recklessness and carelessness	73
Be alert for overly detailed fears	75
Don't downplay the trauma to your child	77
Take some time without the kids	79
Listen for the aftershocks	81
Watch for withdrawal	83
But don't look for school problems afterwards	85
Watch for regression	87
Watch for denial	89
Watch for fear of the future	91
Get professional help	93
Give them something higher to cling to	95
Don't forget to take care of yourself	97
Relish the positives	99
Tailoring to the Age of Your Child	101
Infants	101
Preschoolers	103
Elementary school children	105
Teenagers	107

Answering Children's Questions	109
Mommy, what happened?	109
Will we all die?	111
Why do people have to die, anyway?	113
What does dying feel like?	115
Why did this happen?	117
Will it happen here?	119
Did this happen because I was bad?	121
Can I stay home from school?	123
What about social distancing?	125
Is it ok to cry?	127
Is it ok to laugh and smile?	129
Will there be enough food?	131
What can we do to make a difference?	133
Why am I having bad dreams?	135
Why do I keep thinking about it?	137
Will I ever feel normal again?	139
Writing, Drawing, and Playing as Therapy	141
Writing	143
Drawing	145
Playing	147
For Further Reading	149

Preface

This is the first edition of this book, but unfortunately, likely not to be the last.

Our world has become increasingly global, increasingly inter-connected, increasingly intertwined. Although this has many, many benefits, it also comes at a price.

Everyone who is alive now has been blessed to be living during one of the luckiest times in the history of the world. Most of us are happier, healthier, better educated, better fed, and more secure than people at any other time period. Our grandparents went through widespread disease and world war; our children will likely suffer the effects of global warming. But until now, our generation has been largely unscathed.

But even if we solve it quickly, coronavirus is unlikely to be our last pandemic. Researchers believe that, for a variety of reasons including our interconnectedness, we will now be facing health crises of a magnitude we have not recently encountered. There are many things we can do in response—everything from overhauling our medical system, to working out best guidelines for social interaction.

But most of all, we need to protect our children, who don't have an innate ability to deal with these events. We need to shield them while simultaneously allowing them to actively work through trauma that no one would wish on them. We need to listen to them, and encourage them to talk. We need to comfort them, cuddle them, and hear their fears very carefully. That is what this book is about.

Introduction

As awful a specter as a pandemic is, it is that much worse coupled with children. Children, regardless of the situation, can be nothing but helpless bystanders, buffeted by circumstances.

Yet, if we're careful about our speech and modeling, we can make even a pandemic situation more comprehensible and less frightening for the youngest among us.

Adults, whether they become ill or are quarantined; whether they are gravely sick or are lucky enough to have just a mild case; whether they have suffered economically as a result, or emerge largely unscathed, have a certain amount of life experience that will help most of them get through.

What about the children?

Yet how much worse it is for our children. As adults, we can hear the latest updates and be fearful. But for our children, incomplete understanding coupled with an awareness of our fear and tension, can be terrifying.

For most children, smallpox is an illness from the "old days;" polio is something from their storybooks. Pandemics aren't taught in school. And death is not truly real to children. Until now.

Not only have most of the world's children never experienced a pandemic: They have never experienced the Great Depression, world war, or national trauma of any sort. Although individual children have certainly survived abuse and trauma of various kinds, as a nation, kids today have had the carefree childhood that we barely appreciated in the moment, and can only now look back upon nostalgically and sadly.

And in some ways, the hardest part is watching the rest of us unravel. Accustomed to a routine, to a world that is fairly invariable, children are disturbed by seeing adults everywhere stressed out for reasons they don't fully understand, seeing schools closing but without the usual fun of snow or vacation days, watching their parents fear something they can not really understand and can not see.

Who is this book for?

This book was written to give parents and teachers some guidance in dealing with children and answering their difficult questions during and following a pandemic. There are no perfect answers or solutions to worldwide medical terrors, but this book offers ideas.

It is meant for the many children who may not become ill, but who nonetheless are hearing about the situation non-stop, and are struggling with its implications and the palpable aura of fear it has created.

If your child was in the ICU or hospital, or if you have a close family member who became gravely ill or died, you might want to seek professional counseling for your child. This book, and those listed in the bibliography, may be helpful, but can not replace the interaction with a trained professional grief and trauma therapist.

Remember that even children not directly affected may experience trauma. Studies have shown that both children and adults not physically present at the site of a trauma can later exhibit symptoms of emotional harm; for example, psychiatrists who studied the aftermath of a dam collapse in West Virginia discovered that even those adults not physically in the valley at the time of the flood suffered emotional trauma.

Thus, children who are on the outskirts of a pandemic but see too much coverage on television, for example, may be adversely affected. In addition, traumatic effects may be "contagious" in the sense that they may spread from actual victims to others who were never victims at all.

How is a pandemic different?

One of the key differences is that a pandemic is a group event in a way that kidnappings, abuse, fires, accidents, and hospital operations are not. In some types of trauma, such as abuse, children are singled out for malevolent attention; in others, the trauma is the result of an accident, be it a fire or a car crash. In both situations, the child, or perhaps the child and his immediate family, is the sole object of such attention. The rest of the child's world—his family, his school, or his larger community—are oblivious of, or indifferent to, the trauma that is unfolding.

Of course, this in no way minimizes the effects of such trauma on the individual child and family. Nonetheless, the larger world around them continues to exist unscathed. Although earth-shattering to the child and family involved, such trauma is not a group event.

A pandemic, by contrast, is not specifically directed towards the child himself. One might think the child would therefore feel less singled out, less vulnerable, less personally attacked. Strangely, this is not the case: Merely viewing the events transpiring on television can be traumatic. In fact, studies show that bystanders, both children and adults, are actually *more* likely to be afraid than the primary victims.

In a pandemic, it is not only the child undergoing the trauma: All his communal supports are stressed. His entire lifestyle is under attack. It is his parents, usually the stars he navigates by, who have gone awry and broken down in fear or anger. It is the adults around him who suddenly act strangely. It is his whole neighborhood, city, and country which are suddenly in disarray. It is his routine, the very fabric of his existence, that is uprooted and ignored as everyone is glued to a television set and immersed in worry and anger instead of performing normal roles and rituals.

Because a pandemic is a group event, there is a second impact. Since the family, school, neighborhood, and country are facing the same circumstance, everyone's attention—even that of the children's parents—is diverted from their traumatized children. Parents and teachers experience their own difficulties in dealing with the situation.

Contrast that with other traumatic situations: When your child undergoes a hospital operation, you know you need to be there for him. But when the whole country is reeling under the impact of a pandemic, it's difficult to remember that your child is experiencing the same situation even more acutely.

Parents find it difficult to be there for their children when they themselves are in the midst of the same traumatic circumstances. It's difficult to feel confident, powerful, and in-charge when faced with such terrible events. When you as a parent are immobilized by feelings of helplessness, it is difficult to muster the strength you need to console your child.

Parents are also unprepared for the changes such an incident inflicts on their child. A child who has gone through what we might term *usual* trauma—an operation, a fire, or a car accident, for example—might be cosseted and babied by her parents for weeks or months, in clear acknowledgement that trauma has occurred.

A child who has merely heard radio reports of a pandemic, on the other hand, is often ignored as a serious victim. It is only after their children turn into different children, exhibiting unusual and generally undesirable behavior, that some parents think to question whether it might be trauma.

For your children, this is a horrifying event that they have experienced, and the fact that they have only witnessed it on television or heard about it on the radio in no way lessens the gravity of their loss of security. According to trauma experts, children's feelings of helplessness during a pandemic may cause them to fear loss of family and loss of their own lives, as well as a presentiment that worse things will follow. Although the event itself may resolve, the child's terror lingers.

One final way in which a pandemic is different from most other traumatic situations for children is in the perception of widespread violence and malevolence. When a child is in a car crash, for example, it is probably only that situation—traumatic though it may be—which is frightening. Although a child who is a victim of a car crash may refuse to ride in cars, they probably won't see the whole world through dark glasses.

Contrast that with the child who has experienced a pandemic: In a pandemic situation, it seems that the entire world is to be feared, that nothing, nobody, and nowhere is safe. It is suddenly not the particulars of the given situation, but the whole world that has become dark, gloomy, and full of nasty surprises. The world is no longer a safe place. A pandemic can alter your child's feelings about her life and her world.

Will my child be ok?

It is undeniable that many children will be affected by pandemics. This book gives parents and teachers techniques to minimize its impact.

Ultimately, however, most children are resilient. By all means use the techniques in this book to help your child through these difficult days—but don't spend too much time worrying.

Don't assume that your child's lack of interest is necessarily denial. For many children, the pandemic is mere background noise, completely irrelevant to their lives. Even if your children seem obsessed with the recent news events, don't assume they're traumatized. Kids are emotionally stronger than they look. Your child will probably be fine.

What's inside?

The chapter *Strategies for Helping Your Child* discusses concrete strategies for helping your child during and in the aftermath of a pandemic. It discusses how to handle television and radio reports, how to tailor your emotional response, how to offer reassurance, and how to talk to your children.

It gives specific suggestions for minimizing the impact of a pandemic—keeping to routines, maintaining behavior standards, and the like. It surveys symptoms to watch for in your children such as recklessness, personality changes, and complaints about physical symptoms. It also reminds parents that they need to comfort themselves in this trying time.

The chapter *Tailoring to the Age of Your Child* describes how to talk to your children, based on their age and developmental level. It discusses how infants, preschoolers, grade schoolers and teenagers understand events differently, and how you should tailor your words and actions to each of these age groups.

The chapter *Answering Children's Questions* elaborates on the different questions children will ask in these circumstances. It includes general questions such as "Will it happen here?" and specific questions, such as "What about social distancing?" You'll learn strategies for dealing with your child's reluctance to return to school, his hesitancy to laugh and smile, her worries about dwelling on horrific thoughts, and his fears of never returning to normalcy again.

The chapter *Writing, Drawing, and Playing as Therapy* explores using writing, drawing, and playing as aids to help your child work through the trauma. It gives concrete suggestions of how to encourage your child to explore his feelings by inviting him to draw, write and play. Studies have shown that children who are able to express their fears and inner terrors in these ways bounce back faster.

Finally, the bibliography shares other resources that may be helpful in dealing with a pandemic situation, including books for parents and children on grief, death, and trauma.

Strategies for Helping Your Child

There are no easy answers for how to make everything better while a pandemic is shaking your world, particularly since much of the horror is ongoing. But there are many things you can do and say to help lessen the impact for your children. In employing the specific strategies below, there are a few things to keep in mind.

First, both adults and children are likely to experience some amount of shock and denial during and immediately after a pandemic or other severe trauma. According to the American Psychological Association, these are normal, protective reactions and are likely to be experienced by almost everyone. Your emotional state may be extremely fragile temporarily, leaving you feeling stunned. You and your child may feel unable to internalize that the pandemic is actually occurring.

You may also distance yourself from experiencing the full intensity of the pandemic. You and your child may temporarily feel numb and disconnected from life.

In the days and weeks that follow, you and your child may experience unusually intense emotions, greater irritability, nervous tension, depression, or dramatic mood swings. You may engage in more family fights and conflicts (particularly if children are off school, and you are spending more time closeted up together, in quarantine or not). You or your child may have recurring vivid flashbacks of scenes you've seen on the news, accompanied by sweating, rapid heartbeat, nausea, and chest pain. Normal concentration, sleep, and eating patterns may also be affected.

Be aware that all of these are normal reactions to severe stress, and that with time, the symptoms will lessen. In addition, here are several strategies for helping your child deal with the incident.

Limit television and internet viewing

In the initial stages of a pandemic, try to limit your child's visual exposure to the situation. Pictures are far more disturbing to children, particularly young children, than words.

By limiting television viewing during these situations, and confining yourself to radio and print media, you will go a long way towards limiting the scary pictures that your child will later recall.

Television or internet images of a pandemic, under the best of circumstances, can be scary and repetitive. Under the worst of circumstances, these media may show situations to which you would never willingly subject your child. The trauma of the imagery is certainly more powerful than the same words spoken in a radio report or read aloud from a newspaper.

"We read about the pandemic online, rather than exposing our kids to the television reports," one parent said. "Because of that, I don't think they paid as much attention."

Don't make the mistake of thinking that little children, who may buzz in and out of a room or seem not to be paying attention, are not affected. Their radar is exceptionally tuned for such things, and especially since you will exhibit some emotions while watching, they are sure to be paying attention.

Finally, studies have shown that children who watch a lot of television violence of any sort—whether the disturbing visuals of a pandemic, or even just fictional movies—feel less physically safe than children who watch less violence.

Turn the television off.

Limit your news viewing

Too much watching or listening to the pandemic on the news can lead to feelings of helplessness, lethargy, and despair. In fact, studies show that the news coverage isn't always even an accurate portrayal of a situation. (For example, though statistics may report a decrease in the incidence of crime, reporting of crime in the news has increased.) The more news your child is exposed to, the more helpless and powerless he is likely to feel.

Studies have also shown that traumatic events that occur over an extended period of time may cause greater distress in children than relatively brief events. The longer you leave the news on, and the more nights you watch the news, the longer your child perceives the length of the pandemic.

"It seems like we've been in partial lockdown already for months, even though it's only been days," one mother said.

So try to curtail your news time. Despite the fact that it's somehow mesmerizing to fixate on the radio and listen obsessively as they describe the unfolding latest scenario over and over, it is no healthier for you than it is for your kids. Listen to the news, but set limits on your listening: Try tuning in once a day for updates, rather than leaving the radio on non-stop.

If you have young children, consider listening with headphones. Better yet, if the weather is pleasant bring the radio outside and listen discreetly while they zoom around on bikes or in trees. Children are better able to process horrifying news when they hear about it without the immediacy of television or radio.

In between situations, leave the radio off completely. Make sure you have plenty of "normal" days so that your child's whole world doesn't become news immersion—with all the fear that brings.

Don't let your children listen alone

Don't leave your youngsters listening to the news reports alone. Stay in the room: Your physical presence is calming in such scary times. Staying available to them also means that you can model behavior for them.

Young children, in particular, may not have the verbal capacity to express their feelings, but by keeping them with you while you process the evolving information you can allow them to express themselves physically in your presence.

"My toddler's response is to race around me in circles like a maniac," said a mother of three boys. "He usually runs around the house, but this is his way of discharging some emotion while still being close to me."

Grief therapists, using the work of John Bowlby and Elisabeth Kübler-Ross, name five stages everyone experiences after a bereavement: denial, anger, bargaining, depression, and acceptance. In a pandemic situation, we might add one more: Fear.

Cuddle your children as you hear the news. The physical contact, and the familiar feel of your embrace, will do a great deal to comfort your child.

Slightly older children will be able to obtain access to the news themselves unless you take precautions. Have a frank conversation with your child and explain why you'd like them not to listen to the radio, watch television, or follow it on their phones without you. If you are afraid your child might forget or not listen, consider removing radios, computers, and cellphones for the duration, or at the very least, limiting time.

Exhibit your emotions

Keeping a tight rein on your emotions may be one of the worst things you can do. Children need to see you react. These situations are scary. Respond to that. Sigh. Rant. Cry.

These are normal reactions to extreme stress—and your child needs to see that they are permissible reactions. Otherwise, your child's emotions will stay bottled up inside her—which isn't healthy.

Earl Grollman, national expert on counseling children about death, says that if you repress your feelings, your child is more likely to keep her own emotions at bay. And children are particularly sensitive during a crisis, according to a report by the American Academy of Child and Adolescent Psychiatry. Children receive implicit permission to mourn from adults if they see their adults mourning. Give them that permission.

On the other hand, make sure that your child realizes that although you're sad and angry, you're not angry at *him*. Children often feel responsible for events, but by cuddling them while listening, you can reassure them that your emotions are not directed at them.

You'll also find it healthier for you to allow your emotions to flow naturally, rather than keeping a tight rein on them.

Offer personal reassurance

If it's the truth, stress to your child that although awful, the events are happening to other people, far away. Be emphatic that their immediate support systems—your family, your friends, your neighbors—are safe and sound, and that you'll do your best to keep it that way.

This is important even if you live quite far from the worst of the pandemic. Children are comforted by hearing that their relatives and friends are safe, especially when confronted with such devastation.

Also, point out that even though one area is having a hard time, not all areas are. The point to convey is that bad things only happen once in a very long while, not all the time, everywhere.

If far away, make sure that your child knows where the events occurred. Most young children don't have a clear sense of physical distance. It may be very helpful to your child to understand how far away your town is from Italy or China. Expressing the distance in time ("It would take me 65 days and a boat to get there if we started right now") rather than mileage which they don't understand, is helpful for young children.

"Oh, that's where we went on vacation last year," said one four year old of the situation in Italy. "That's very far away."

On the other hand, don't expect that your reassurances will magically solve your child's problems. Just because you tell them that they're safe, your children's fears may not evaporate. Cynthia Monahon, in her book *Children and Trauma: A Guide for Parents and Professionals* calls children's memories of trauma "tyrannical" and points out that healing takes time.

Keep to your routine

Keep the children's routine as close to usual as possible. Obviously if everyone in the house is home listening to the radio then your child can't be at his violin lesson, and if schools are closed it will be hard to maintain the routine. But varying children's routines—even for happy occasions like vacations—can be disorienting for them. Everyone knows that infants and toddlers do best with a "regular" naptime and bedtime; routines of some sort are equally important to older children. In pandemic situations this is even more true.

"Our kids seemed pretty upset, but we had dinner as a family and then story time, and by bedtime they seemed fine."

Studies have shown that the child's perception of the outcome of the situation affects their distress level. Children whose lives are negatively altered after the initial events suffer greater distress than children who view the event as one isolated negative blip on the horizon. So try to keep to your regular routine, in the hope that this normalcy will keep the situation contained.

Try to remember to make time for meals, and have them in the same place as usual; read the same goodnight stories, and conduct the bedtime ritual you always do. These routines will help your child orient himself and calm his feelings of the world being out of whack. Routines are a familiar haven in a sea of strangeness.

And don't forget to make some time for family fun, despite the events of the world, in whatever ways you're able to without violating rules. Children need fun in their lives, regardless of the world situation.

Talk to your children

Children need to hear you process the situation—so they know what to make of it. By talking to your child as an incident is occurring, you bring them into the experience with you, rather than leaving them puzzled and alone on the periphery. Let them know that you are worried and saddened.

But don't overdo your explanations, either.

"I was thinking I should explain the whole thing to them," said one father. "But I don't understand it myself—how could they?"

Admit to your child that these are difficult issues, and that sometimes it's hard to know how to think about things like this. Some problems don't have easy answers, and children do better if their adults admit that, rather than trying to give pat answers that don't satisfy.

If you have opinions on the politics of the situation, or ideas on how the government should respond, share those thoughts with your children. Such conversations will help them feel included—and empowered.

Talk at your child's level

Consider the age of your child. For example, infants pick up on the anxieties and actions of those around them and may be fussier than is usual. Try to be calm when interacting with your infant, and keep their routine the same.

For toddlers, keeping their routines is paramount. If they ask questions, make sure you answer simply and tell them that you'll keep them safe.

"My kids just wanted to stay close by me all day," said one parent.

Preschoolers don't understand a lot of what is happening. For example, most preschoolers do not understand that death is permanent; they think of it as a vacation that someone comes back from. Make sure you spend the time to deal with their questions and misperceptions.

Preschoolers, in particular, may have a difficult time because of their inability to separate reality from fantasy. According to Joanne Cantor, author of

Mommy, I'm Scared — How TV and Movies Frighten Children and What We Can Do To Protect Them, preschoolers are as terrified when Pinocchio turns into a donkey as they are by a story on a school shooting. Particularly after experiencing the heightened emotions of everyone around them during a pandemic, your preschooler may think that *everything* on television is real.

School age children are more interested in the events that are happening, but are less capable than older children of communicating. Reassure them that your family will be safe.

Contrary to what you might assume, teenagers particularly need the presence of an adult, because they will understand the situation enough to be terrified. Share your feelings with them honestly, and encourage them to share theirs.

And let them talk to you

Sometimes the best way for children to process such a situation is to talk about it. Let them. Do not force them to talk if they are not ready. But try not to shut down such conversations, if they start, even though you may feel uneasy and not know quite what to say. Ask open-ended, rather than yes/no questions, to try to elicit things that might otherwise stay buried.

"I thought my kids were ok with it, because I asked them and they said they were fine," one mother confided. "Then I read something that suggested asking what color they felt the world was this week. And two of them said black! And then the whole thing came pouring out—a lot more anxiety than I would have known about otherwise."

Ask what your child already knows. This way you can clarify distortions, and help the child get accurate information. How many 4-year-olds really understand what a pandemic is? But don't be too quick to jump in with advice and information. Wait to find out what your child is feeling before offering an opinion.

Also, make sure that each child has some alone time with you. If they seek you out while you're doing the dishes or at your computer, make the time for them that moment: Later they might be unable to verbalize what they wanted to share. Be alert for times when they are more likely to talk.

Try to concentrate your talking time in the earlier parts of the day. Discussing the pandemic right before bedtime is a surefire way to encourage nightmares. Instead, use the time before bed to read a comforting book, play a board game, or simply spend some time cuddling. Talk in the morning; snuggle at night. (And stay off devices right before bedtime: Studies have shown that device use before bedtime impedes sleeping.)

And let them say what they want

Children can have strong feelings, sometimes exceedingly unpleasant feelings. If, in the weeks after the pandemic starts, you allow your child to express himself as he likes, without censure or judgment, it will prevent his feelings from being expressed in more disturbing behaviors, and he will heal faster.

Your child may also have scary fantasies that he elaborates in gory detail. As long as he is not acting on these fantasies, accept them as part of his healing process, disturbing though they may be.

Or your child may have particularly sad and gloomy feelings, which may be difficult for you to hear.

One mother told me, "I thought my nine-year-old was oblivious to the whole situation. And then when I tucked him in, he said his prayers and added 'And please God, protect us against coronavirus' in his prayers."

Let your child verbalize the situation as he needs to, whatever expression that takes. If he wants to talk about it with you, encourage him, whether or not you like how he is talking.

If you're uncomfortable with how an older child is talking about the situation, it's ok to admit that. Saying something like, "I understand how strongly you feel about this, though it makes me sad to hear you talk about the world that way," is ok for your child to hear; chances are they'll see it in your face whether or not you verbalize it. But make sure your child understands that even though his thoughts may occasionally make you uncomfortable, you still want to hear them.

"I'm sorry the world is making you feel so sad right now, but I'm glad we can talk about it," one mother told her daughter.

Don't lie to your children

Don't be dishonest in answering your children's questions. If they ask if people died, admit the truth. But don't go into more details than they are interested in, either: Don't volunteer this information unless they ask you. Listen carefully to be sure you are only answering what they want to hear.

"Our seven-year-old asked what was going on. We said we were listening to sad news. She didn't want to hear the details," said one mother.

When children perceive the event—correctly or incorrectly—as life threatening to them, they feel more disruption than when they perceive it as a removed threat. Thus, without lying about the details, attempt to in some way "remove" the danger by indicating its remoteness.

Stressing that you are all safe is comforting. Often, just your willingness to listen to their fears will help them.

The more honest you are in general in conversations with your children, the better-equipped they are to handle this sort of extreme situation. If you talk in euphemisms about death and prevent them from going to funerals, they will have a far different perception of reality than a child who knows that "Grandpa died," and can relate details of the funeral he attended. Honesty in advance pays off in extreme situations.

Understand that you are not sparing your children by lying to them either about death in general or the particulars of the situation. Stating a falsehood that your children must later unlearn is helpful to no one.

On the other hand, make sure that your comments are age appropriate. In the same way that you wouldn't share certain details of sex or money with younger children, you don't need to share all the details of a pandemic.

Finally, do not use the euphemism "sleep" in referring to the dead. Otherwise you may well create a dread of bedtimes, with your child afraid that if he falls asleep, he may never awaken.

Convey a sense of hope

Regardless of the sadness of the particular situation, it's important that children retain a sense of hope and optimism about the world in general. Even in the most dire of circumstances, look for the silver lining in the clouds.

Stress the positives in the situation: Isn't it a lucky thing this happened when it wasn't busy tourist season in the most affected places?

Studies have shown that when the trauma involves human malevolency (such as an assault), rather than natural forces (such as accidents or hurricanes), children are affected more negatively, as are we all. So stress that part of the story: This isn't like a war, everyone's together and fighting this as a group.

Mention all the many examples of people going out of their way to help: Point out the many giving blood and donations, the many showing support for neighbors and total strangers.

Encourage children to participate in something that will give the situation some meaning, or will actively help victims: Go to a blood drive with your child, go to an (online) prayer meeting or community support meeting, or take up a neighborhood collection to raise funds for the affected families.

"We helped convince people to donate blood for the blood drive!" one eight-year-old informed me gleefully. It was clear that being able to take action had lessened the impact of the situation for him, and given him renewed faith in the humanity of the people around him.

And whatever your personal convictions about the likelihood of more bad news, don't share this with your child. You need to be honest about facts and events that have occurred, but there is nothing for your child to gain from hearing your gloomy speculation. For that matter, it won't help you either: Think positive!

Be patient

Stressful situations require healing time. Be patient with your child, and be patient with yourself. Allow everyone the freedom to repeat the events of the experience as often as necessary.

"She keeps talking about what's happening," one mother told me. "It's as if she can discharge it if she keeps repeating it. But I'm also discussing it non-stop."

Stressful events that last a long time and pose a great threat, and where significant loss of life is involved, take longer to resolve than shorter, less intense situations.

And stressful situations that are clumped together—such as a pandemic where a lot of countries are involved—are more disturbing still. Expect to spend more time than you might think healing.

A natural disaster like this can loom large in the eyes of children. Give them the patient support and comfort they need to process the experience, again and again not just in the days during, but in the months after as well. Children are extraordinarily resilient and they will heal eventually—but like any wound, it takes time.

Give them options

One thing children need in order to feel better after an event like this is to recapture some of the power that the situation drained from them. Feeling helpless is an emotionally hazardous condition if it persists, and restoring your child's sense of empowerment is one of the easiest things you can do for them.

Since you're obviously unable to give them a sense of power over the events of the pandemic, enable them in other ways. Giving them options lets them feel they have some control over their lives and restores a sense of power over their daily existence.

Give them choices about what they'd like for dinner, or where they'd like to go for a walk outside. Ask them what they'd like to do during the weekend, or where you should go on a family outing or vacation when the situation is all over. Even if your child is a toddler, you can let her pick her own outfit in the morning, or choose when to have her snack.

Another idea is to go through old family photo albums or their baby album, and point out all the different choices and decisions they've made throughout their lives. "See, here's where you wanted to go for your birthday party. Look, this is the dress you picked out – you wore it every day for weeks!"

Reminding them of how much control they have over their lives and experiences will be subtly empowering and much appreciated.

Let them be helpful

Just as children respond well to choices, because they find it empowering, likewise children are comforted by helping out.

According to Mary Ann and James Emswiler, authors of *Guiding Your Child Through Grief,* children report feeling comforted by helping out. Helping gives children a sense of self-esteem and a sense of control over a situation, and in that way it's quite empowering.

Helping out, like having options, gives your child a sense of control over the situation and their lives, control which a pandemic takes from them. Helping out can help your child reassert his feelings of control and power, and take back the situation.

"I thought they were being nice, but then I realized helping out was making *them* feel better," said one astonished mother.

So even if your children don't ask for tasks—and many won't—look for opportunities for them to help. Ask them to fetch items from another part of the house for you. Have them help to entertain a younger sibling. Engage them in cleaning up or cooking with you.

Most children are happy to help in short doses anyway, because of the responsibility helping gives them. Particularly during a pandemic, it can be important in reestablishing their sense of control and empowerment. This is one case where helpful children are happy children.

Enhance their self esteem

It is also useful for parents to remind their children about their strengths and skills. This will help to combat the helplessness that children often feel during a situation like a pandemic.

Talk about what they do well and all the problems and difficult situations they have solved in the past. Remind them of their strengths and the many things over which they have mastery.

Again, this might be a good opportunity to pull out the old family photo albums and remind your child of how many things she has mastered over the years and how much she has learned. "Look, here's a picture of you tying your shoes. You were so happy when you figured out how to do that. Here's one of you learning to whistle. Here's a photo of you on your first pony ride."

Skills are a concrete manifestation of mastery over their lives, and children need to be reminded that they are not helpless, that they have expertise and power.

"I commented on how nicely Mary was learning to ride her bicycle," one mother noted. "I didn't think it was such a big deal, but she puffed up proudly and enumerated a whole list of other things she could do well. She was much cheerier the rest of the day."

It's important for children to feel some amount of control over themselves and their destinies, and the self esteem that goes along with it.

Make lists

Therapists who work with grief report that making lists can be therapeutic. Writing a list of things to do, for example, can be grounding and keep you focused. And writing lists can restore a sense of normalcy that is severely lacking during a pandemic or any other trauma. Finally, though you may feel emotionally fragile and exhausted, making a list can be energizing and uplifting.

Lists can also give children a sense of future and hope for "later" which can be lacking following a pandemic situation. Doing some concrete planning for later or even adult life can counteract their pessimism.

So make lists with your children of things you're grateful for, or happy about. Include talking to friends, music, playing with puppies, hugs, getting a birthday present, sitting in front of a woodstove, and playing on the beach.

And make lists of things connected to you and your child's future. Plan the details of a vacation.

Prepare for an upcoming milestone birthday party. Make a to-do list of all the skills you want to learn or the places you want to go in the next five or ten years.

Make a fantasy list with your child of where they want to be when they are adults: Where they want to live, in what kind of a house, with how many children of their own, doing what sort of work, etc.

Make it a game and see who can come up with the largest and most interesting list of things that are good in your life. This is a fun activity even under normal circumstances; during a pandemic, it can be both grounding and cheering.

Maintain your children's behavior standards

During a pandemic, some children's behavior will disintegrate. Between the stress of hearing the news, the stress of watching adults falling apart, the children's change in routine and often lack of school, and the general climate of uneasiness, many children will find it difficult to follow the normal rules and maintain their usual standards of behavior.

On the one hand, you need to cut the kids a little slack: We're all a little stressed out, and you need to understand that children's behavior may suffer in subtle or not-so-subtle ways. This isn't the time to quibble over every little outburst or infraction.

On the other hand, you need to maintain the usual rules of the house and the usual expectations of your child.

"This is a very sad week, but we still need to do homework," one mother firmly told her children to their dismay.

Expectations are part of what makes your children's world secure. Don't upset their precarious sense of security even more by suddenly letting them do as they like. Continue to enforce household and family rules.

Some parents may find it easiest to be frank with their children: "I know this is a difficult time, and everything seems topsy-turvy," one mother confided to her three children. "But we're going to keep everything as normal as possible because it will make us all feel better. And that means that you're going to have to do all your regular things—like cleaning your room—and follow all the regular house rules—like going to bed at your regular time."

Altering behavior standards for abnormal situations will only serve to further unnerve your already anxious children: Keep to your regular rules and standards. Parental expectations are comforting.

Understand sleep patterns may change

Be aware that sleep patterns are likely to change. Sleep is always affected by stress: Even going on vacation or having guests can result in sleepless nights. Children like their routines, and just the slightest change can affect their sleep patterns.

All the more so when the child and your family are in the midst of a pandemic. Your child may be reluctant to go to sleep alone. He may want to snuggle into your bed or at least your bedroom. He may want more "tuck-ins" than usual, or ask you to check on him more often. His sleep patterns may change, resulting in later nights and earlier mornings.

You might well see an increase in nightmares, which can be terrifying for your child, as they can be interspersed with bits of the actual trauma situation. Or they may be peppered with his waking worries, and he may tell you he dreamed of losing you or being alone or in danger.

Even older children and teenagers may experience disruptions in their sleeping, or may feel scared about sleeping alone. You may hear older children who've been sleeping in attic rooms asking to return to the rooms of their childhood, or children who've been sleeping alone for years requesting a move to a room with siblings. Or your children may not be sleeping at all.

"No one is sleeping well," said one exhausted mother, "And that includes the kids. I don't want them to move into our bedroom, but I'm wondering if that might make more sense than just spending the night running back and forth to them."

Be there for your child during his disturbed nights, and don't spend too much time worrying that things will never return to normal. Remember to show a lot of physical comfort during the day and before bedtime, be available to talk during waking hours, and above all exercise patience. This won't last forever.

Be alert for personality changes

In the same way that sleep patterns may change during a pandemic, you may see subtle, or not so subtle, personality changes in your child. These personality changes are unlikely to be permanent, but they may be worrisome nonetheless.

Your child's thoughts, attitudes, and relations to people may change. This can take all different forms: They may seem quieter or noisier, worried or silly, introverted or wild. You may see more aggressive play, more anxiety about strangers, or louder and more boisterous behavior.

In teenagers you may see more cynicism or sarcasm. You are also likely to notice them taking a sudden intense interest in world events and the news, as a way of keeping a sense of control over the situation.

But even very young children can be affected by the upheaval of basic expectations about their world.

"My five year old just became much quieter than usual. Very shy, very timid, very silent. As though he was suddenly tentative about his life," one mother told us.

You may see an erosion of your child's trust in the goodness of people. You may experience your child's decreased feelings of safety. You may see selfish, preoccupied behavior, suspicion, or pessimism.

See it for what it is, and don't dwell on it: It's likely to be temporary. Envelope your child in warmth and love.

Watch for anger

Among the personality changes or new attitudes that you might see in your child is sudden or increased anger. Unless the anger is harmful to your child or others, this can be a very healing emotion, although it may be difficult to live with.

Keep in mind that anger, in particular, can be a cover for other, more complicated emotions. If you notice that your child seems unusually angry, or is behaving more aggressively than is usual, there's a good chance that she feels scared and helpless.

"The kids have been much more physical with each other than usual, and much rougher," one parent noted.

Remember to comfort your child often, whether he seems to need it or not. "Tough" emotions may just be a cover for real fear and concern. Or it may not be a cover for anything—it may simply be anger. Give frequent hugs, and be available to talk to your child.

Parents often find it difficult to see their children expressing anger. Our tendency is to distract them or rebuke them. Forcing your child to contain his emotions, however, is the worst thing you can do if you want to move past the incident.

As long as the anger is not harmful to the child or others, it is a positive thing. Remember that any expression of emotion, including anger, is a healing, empowering experience.

So watch your child's anger without reprimand, and show your love and comfort in as many ways as you can.

Listen for complaints of bruises

You might not think that your child's sudden preoccupation with a skinned knee is related to a pandemic—but you'd be wrong.

Worries of bumps or bruises, or complaints of pain or fatigue are all stress or trauma reactions. Particularly for a child who finds it difficult—because of age or emotional development—to verbalize his emotional fragility or fear, complaints of bruising can be a way of attracting parental attention for a hurt that is not actually physical.

Your child may exhibit a sudden new concern about her cut knees and skinned shins, or react disproportionately to a minor bump. She may complain of tummy ache or headache. She may experience rashes, lethargy, nausea, colds, weakness, forgetfulness, or cramps. Be alert for such talk particularly if your child is usually not a complainer.

One parent noticed that her six-year-old seemed upset about the scrape on his knee, and that her teen had a stomach ache.

These complaints are a way for your child to say, "I'm hurting inside" without the necessity of vocalizing it. Younger children may take this tact because of the difficulty in verbalizing their complicated emotions; older children may exhibit the same symptoms because of embarrassment of discussing what's really bothering them. Or they may complain of bruising or pain without understanding that they're really experiencing emotional fragility and anxiety.

Either way, take their concerns seriously and comfort their tears. Even if the hurt strikes you as a minor nothing, be aware that it probably masks a deeper emotional wound, and tend to it accordingly.

Such physical manifestations may continue for weeks. Listen to the complaints, and be appropriately sympathetic. By comforting the alleged physical manifestation of what is actually a psychological internal hurt, you'll be healing both.

Watch for recklessness and carelessness

Another manifestation of such situations is daredevil behavior and recklessness. It's unclear whether the child is acting this way in despair at the situation, or whether it's an attempt at self-injury so they can be returned to the safety of their mother.

In fact, children who are engaging in such incautious behavior may themselves be unaware of what they are doing.

If you see your child preparing to jump out of a tree or engage in other unusual, risky behavior, take precautions.

Be particularly alert since you don't want to be in the emergency room unnecessarily during this overcrowded hospital period.

And if you see a pattern of such behavior, get professional counseling for your child at once.

Be alert for overly detailed fears

If your child's worries about the situation seem particularly graphic and realistic to you, take note.

According to Dr. Lenore Terr, author of *Too Scared to Cry: How trauma affects children...and ultimately us all,* once a fear sounds very literal and very specific there is a strong possibility that actual experience underlies the fear.

She notes that while many developing youngsters develop a fear of dogs, they fear all of them—not just large ones with white spots. If the fear is that specific, it is likely to be the result of a specific experience.

If your child's details of the pandemic while playing or in conversation sound too real to you, or in some way too graphic or explicit, try to initiate a conversation with your child to get at the underlying fear.

It is possible that your child misunderstood something he heard on the radio or from his friends, and that his fear stems from something that you might be able to put to rest. Young children, in particular, are quite capable of misunderstanding the conversations and news reports they hear—which may make the situation more frightening than it need be.

In any case, discussing the details of the situation, if your child is already aware of them anyway, will help to soften the reality. And parental participation in discussing the fear will probably make it less scary for your child.

So talk it through with your child—and talk it through again, as often as necessary.

Don't downplay the trauma to your child

One thing almost every parent succumbs to, in the aftermath of a trauma such as this, is the inclination to play down the effects to her child.

It is tempting for parents to conclude, after the immediate situation is over, that their child hasn't suffered from the incident.

"After all," one mother told me, "She never had coronavirus! None of us did. She just heard about it like everyone else. Why is she going on about it all the time?"

Surprisingly, research has shown that mere witnesses to a violent or traumatic incident or event are actually more likely to turn violent in the future as a result of their experience than the primary victims of the attack.

It is, in fact, the mere bystanders who are most adversely affected. And that means that your child, who thankfully was *not* directly involved in the situation, can be most affected.

Moreover, those who were not directly endangered can be as emotionally harmed as those who were there, according to other studies.

So your child who only *saw* details of the pandemic on television may be as wounded emotionally as had she been physically ill.

By processing their feelings and receiving the comfort of their loved ones after witnessing such an event, you can reduce the likelihood of permanent scarring. So treat your child's intensity around the events seriously.

Take some time without the kids

Make sure you spend some time processing your own feelings about the events, without your children around.

A pandemic is frightening for adults, as well as children. You may fear for your own personal safety, and that of your family. You may experience the same feelings of panic and anxiety that you need to look for in your child.

The situation may also renew old feelings of loss or bereavement that you need to work through. It may bring back an adult's feelings of terror that were experienced in a war. It may bring feelings of loss that were experienced after the death of a loved one. Or it may bring other, seemingly unrelated memories, needs, or emotional hurts from childhood that should be resolved.

You need to spend some time resolving those feelings of grief when you are not in the presence of your children.

That might mean going for a walk by yourself just to think about things, keeping a journal, or talking about the situation with a friend or a therapist.

In addition, couples need to spend time with each other. The stress the situation puts on individuals can have detrimental effects on family relationships if not carefully managed, and you don't want to put further stress on your children by adding the burden of forcing them to listen to your fighting.

So spend some time together doing something fun or relaxing. Take a walk, play a board game, read aloud to each other. Try not to spend all the time discussing the situation. Do *not* spend your time together listening to the news!

Listen for the aftershocks

Pay careful attention to your child's behavior. Is she moody? More lethargic than usual? Poorly behaved? Eating less? Listless?

Any of these symptoms might be a clue that she was very shaken by the situation and needs to process it more completely.

Try doing something active together: Plant a garden, exercise, play a game. Encouraging your children to express themselves through art, music, drama, puppetry, or writing can be a way for children to make themselves heard, and is often less threatening to children than verbalizing what they're feeling.

On the other hand, when a parent's worry about a child's reaction is excessive, the parent's very anxiety can overwhelm the child with despair. Don't burden your child with fears that are unnecessary. Take a one-day-at-a-time approach, and try not to worry compulsively about your child unless it seems warranted.

Watch for withdrawal

Be alert for signs that your child is withdrawing from the world. For your child, the world used to be a safe, secure place. Suddenly, the world has become scary. And faced with a suddenly scary world, withdrawal may seem the safest approach to your child. It is, above all, fear of being further (unhappily) surprised by more bad news that your child wants to avoid.

Some children will try to make the world feel safer by holding back on their activities: Avoiding rough play, distancing from friends, and abdicating from any activities that might trigger a memory of the incident are all ways of withdrawing. And by withdrawing, your child lessens the chance that she will be surprised again by something scary. This fear of future fear can immobilize children.

"It's as if she's withholding herself from the world now that it's proven itself to be an unsafe place," one father said sadly. "I long for the old rough-and-tumble interactions."

Encourage your child gradually to participate in her former activities. Don't lecture, but do provide gentle support.

Ultimately, your child needs to realize that her behavior and activities will not affect the world situation or her personal situation, and that resuming her normal routines afterwards will not put her at additional risk of trauma.

But this is something that's more easily preached than practiced. So be encouraging, and be patient.

But don't look for school problems afterwards

Although you may notice changes of all sorts in your child in the months following a pandemic, the one that you probably won't see is deteriorating performance in school.

Studies, both of recent immigrant children who had experienced traumatic situations, and of kidnapped children, reveal that traumatic situations do not usually have a negative effect on school performance.

Even a psychically traumatized child can work hard in school, behave normally in school, and get grades consistent with their performance before the trauma.

School is an organizing structure, so the fact that kids do ok in school isn't surprising. Under most circumstances, children will keep it together at school—and then fall apart at home, where it's "safe" to do so.

Consistently, do not assume that your child is *not* affected just because their school behavior and performance has remained stable.

Asking your child's teacher for opinions on whether the situation has unduly affected your child, therefore, is insufficient, because your child may not be exhibiting the extent of his uneasiness at school—only at home.

In such situations, it is more likely to be children's *home* behaviors that are an indicator of problems, not school behaviors.

So watch what is happening at home.

Watch for regression

Watch your child for behavioral regression.

Children under stress typically respond with a temporary lapse in age-appropriate behavior. In the same way that bringing a newborn into the house may mean your three year old is suddenly back in diapers, in the aftermath of the pandemic you may find all your children behaving suddenly younger than their ages.

Regression is one way for upset children to cope. You may see thumb sucking, toilet accidents, and the like.

By returning to a younger stage, your child is forcing you to respond as when the child was younger and needier.

One parent confided that her child, toilet-trained for a year, is suddenly wetting the bed again.

This is a natural response to stress, and for many children, an inevitable one. Respond by treating the child as if he *were* the younger age he is attempting to recapture, and provide lots of extra love and warmth.

And don't worry: This behavior won't last forever.

Watch for denial

Confronted with a single, horrifying event, adults often react with denial, whereby they consciously prevent themselves from thinking about the incident, and disbelieve its reality.

Children, on the other hand, faced with a single traumatic event, remember the horror with clarity.

However, confronted with numerous instances of disaster, or a series of horrors, a child will brace for shock and start ignoring the reality. Repeated disasters encourage denial in children. And denial—under certain circumstances such as these—is not necessarily an unhealthy thing.

If your child is in denial about the pandemic, and refuses to admit that anything bad happened, he may have been strongly affected by the circumstances, and you may need to watch him carefully to make sure he's recovering.

But just because he's not talking about it doesn't mean that he's in denial: It's also possible that it just hasn't appeared on his radar screen.

If your child seems unaffected by events, uninterested in discussing the situation, and generally immune to what's going on around him, don't assume there's a problem. Make note of it, and pay attention to see if anything further develops over time.

Watch for fear of the future

Children who have been affected by a scary event, such as a pandemic, may express concerns about all sorts of things, and exhibit all sorts of out-of-the-ordinary behavior.

Even if your child is expressing concerns about lack of a future—or if questioned, cannot seem to conceive of having a future—don't worry. Fear of the future is likely to be just a temporary reaction to such a situation.

Even teenagers can suddenly exhibit fear-of-the-future.

Much more worrisome than a temporary inability to plan for the future is a chronic hopelessness or despair that would indicate a serious depression.

If your child's hopelessness continues, monitor her closely; if it does not disappear over time, and your child seems to be falling into a prolonged depression, seek counseling.

Get professional help

If your child is generally resilient and able to cope with emotionally challenging situations, she will be more likely to bounce back after the pandemic is over. If you have a child who finds such situations challenging in general, he may be more at risk.

Be aware that there is an anxiety condition called post-traumatic stress disorder (PTSD) that can occur after witnessing a terrifying event. In adults, the condition can cause flashbacks and frightening memories of the traumatic event.

In children, it is more likely to manifest as obsessive play about the incident. This disorder can and does occur to children who have seen violent imagery on television: It is not necessary that they actually have been in the situation themselves. Even if they were never ill or in quarantine, they may have PTSD.

According to the American Psychological Association, "Continued and aggressive emotional outbursts, serious problems at school, preoccupation with the traumatic event, continued and extreme withdrawal, and other signs of intense anxiety or emotional difficulties all point to the need for professional assistance."

Bear in mind that symptoms can often erupt months after the event. If you suspect your child's behavior is post-traumatic stress disorder, seek counseling.

Support groups may also be useful to children who do not seem to be recovering. Often, just realizing that others are still caught in the same morass of feelings can be helpful to children and adults alike.

Give them something higher to cling to

Don't let the situation shatter your child's faith—be it in God, or in humankind. If you believe in God, admit that it's hard to know how to reconcile that with a tragedy of this proportion. Tell your child that sometimes what God does is baffling and incomprehensible.

And belief in God does not necessarily mean that you always understand why God does what he does.

"We compared it to the Holocaust. We know God is there—but sometimes we don't understand why he allows what he allows," said one mother. "It's not a great answer, but it's hard to reconcile God with so much mayhem."

Admit your confusion and sadness, but don't forget to point out the good things, the silver lining, and the shows of support and valor that are all around us in trying times.

If you have any affiliation with a church or synagogue, now is a great time to pursue that. Sharing such a situation with a community of like-minded people, even virtually, can be incredibly supportive and comforting, for both your child and you.

Don't attempt to feed your child platitudes about God unless you believe them; he won't be fooled if you're sprouting a party line that you don't believe.

But don't allow your own doubts and skepticism to prevent your child from being comforted, either. God means different things to different people, and your child may very well find solace in a God that watches over him personally, whether or not you truly believe in a personal God.

Don't forget to take care of yourself

One of the problems inherent in extreme trauma is that parents, deluged with concern for their children, forget that they themselves also underwent the trauma.

One parent confided that she had no time to worry about herself, she was so focused on her children.

Don't neglect your child, but don't neglect yourself either. You are also shaken, worried, and depressed. We all are. And we all need some extra love and comfort for the days ahead.

Expect less of yourself in the next days. You may feel tired, lethargic, and unable to accomplish anything. You may feel exhausted and sleep-deprived. Don't worry if you feel distracted and unable to cope. These are natural outcomes and will be alleviated over time.

And don't forget to take care of yourself. Try to get enough sleep, and try to eat well-balanced regular meals. (Remember to "put your own oxygen mask on first".)

Reach out to people more than you might normally—stop and talk to the neighbors; call friends who are long-distance. Fostering a sense of community during difficult times makes us all feel less alone.

And remember to stop and smell the roses.

In the wake of a something like this, it's human nature to feel survivor guilt and attempt to curtail your pleasures. But happiness isn't a betrayal of those who died. Glory in the wonder of being alive, and enjoy it with your child, family, and community.

Relish the positives

Ironically, some parents find trauma can be a positive thing. It's hard to believe, but it can be true: Trauma can sometimes clarify your priorities.

One father said, "One thing that has done is made us rethink things. There are no big deals anymore."

So take the opportunity the situation affords to spend more time together as a family, let go of the minor nuisances, and cherish the important things in life.

Tailoring to the Age of Your Child

Before you begin answering children's questions about a pandemic, you need to think carefully about the developmental level of your child. Children understand events at their level and through the lens of their experiences. As parents, we need to talk to our children openly, honestly, but in a way that will help them understand what they need to know—without unnecessarily frightening them.

Approach conversations with your children in the same way that you would approach conversations about sex and money: Certain information is appropriate for certain ages.

Infants

Although infants are pre-verbal, they are intuitively aware of the emotions of the people around them. They will notice instantly that you are smiling less, playing differently or not at all, and generally not there for them in your usual way. Infants whose parents are upset have difficult eating and sleeping; have a tendency to cry more; and are generally "fussier" than usual. Your infant will certainly pick up on your emotions.

As much as possible, soothe your infant by keeping him close. Keep to his regular schedule, and try to make up in physical solace what you are unable to give in emotional constancy. Expect your infant to be as irritable and emotionally fragile as everyone else in the family during these difficult days, and be patient.

Preschoolers

Preschoolers, though verbal, are obviously too young to appreciate the real significance of a pandemic. At this age, children are only interested in the world as it relates to their own experiences. They will be particularly interested in the sights that they understand on television. They don't have much of an understanding of death at this age, and often think of it as a temporary condition.

Because he doesn't understand that death is a permanent condition, your preschooler may not understand why everyone is so sad and worried.

You need to make sure your preschooler knows what's happening to some extent, because he is sure to hear about the pandemic even if he's not at school and even if you don't personally tell him. On the other hand, if he doesn't ask, you don't need to tell them all the dismaying details. Simply say something like, "There's a sickness going around, and people in other parts of the world are getting sick." If he asks for further details, provide them, but be sure you are only answering his questions rather than giving him more information than he needs.

You will probably find that your preschooler will want to talk about what happened again and again. Let him. Healing will occur faster for an upset child if he is able to continue to rehash the situation. Drawing, drama, and writing can be helpful as well; see the chapter *Writing, Drawing, and Playing as Therapy* for more information on using these activities as therapy.

When listening to news reports, be sure to assure your child that your emotional reaction and worry have nothing to do with him. Children of this age feel guilt for a great many things, and if they see your response they may assume it's directed towards them. Cuddle your preschooler in your lap while listening to the news so that he is comforted and realize your strain is directed elsewhere.

Elementary school children

Six to twelve year olds are at a developmental level that enables them to understand events outside their direct experience, though they still will have little grasp of the ramifications. You need to be especially honest with your child of this age: She is old enough to access the information elsewhere (by interrogating other children, for example) yet still be confused about implications.

A simple explanation for this age group is probably best. Try something like, "Something terrible happened today. More people died in a faraway place." Explain that that's why you've been listening to the radio so much. Stress that your family is safe. Then wait for her to ask you questions. You might also want to talk to her about positive steps you will take, such as donating blood to people who need it, or raising money to help the people who were affected.

Although they technically understand death, children under the age of about nine think that death is something that only happens to old people. Thus, the reality of hearing about younger people's deaths may disturb them, or they may not internalize it. A slightly older child will understand that death is possible even for younger people, and will be aware of his own mortality, though usually he will be in denial about this.

Remember, also, to reassure children that your home is safe, and that the rest of the family will be safe.

Teenagers

Teenagers will be getting a lot of their information about the pandemic from outside the home. They are also at a developmental level sufficient to understand the significance of the event. Finally, teens will realize that there is a possibility of further death in a way that a younger child will not.

Despite the fact that your teenagers may already know about the situation, make sure you process it with them. Talk to them and allow time in the next weeks for them to talk to you. Don't assume that they don't need to talk about it and that they're handling their emotions well. Some adolescents may be scared to discuss the situation, some may seem fine and uninterested in the discussion, and others will be brash in their assurances that they are not scared, but fear is at the root of all of these responses. Find the time to talk.

Answering Children's Questions

Mommy, what happened?

Start by hugging your child. When she says she wants to know what happened, what she's really asking for is to be protected from the scary events, and to be safe.

Tell her that you don't know exactly what happened. It's the truth: A lot of the initial information is just plain wrong, and is later rescinded; point that out to your child. (That's the downside of listening to the news as it is happening; the news is a lot more accurate, as well as a lot more bearable, well after the event.)

Do say that people are ill if that much is clear, and that you are sad. Your child will certainly realize that you are upset, and it's better for her to hear it from you directly.

Make sure she realizes that your worry and grief are not directed at her, however. Cuddle and comfort her physically so she internalizes that.

As events unfold, you can give your child more information, as much as you think is age-appropriate. But don't overburden her with more than she really asks to know. And keep her close and cuddled: By asking you questions, children are really seeking reassurance that they are safe and protected.

Will we all die?

Keep in mind that *how* you answer this question is as important as what you say. If your child senses that you are terrified and out of control, she won't believe your verbal reassurance. Try to aim for sadness, rather than despair.

Stress that your family is safe. That's really what your child is most concerned about: Death of strangers, especially if your children are sheltered from watching the visual images on television, is not nearly as disturbing to children as upsetting the sanctity of their loved ones.

If the events happened in what is still a distant locale for you, explain how far away that is in a way even your littlest child can understand: "It would take us 45 days to walk from here to there. That's very far away."

If your child and family believes in God or another higher being, you can tell your child that it is your job as a parent to keep her safe, and it is God's job to keep your whole family and community safe.

Now is a good time to revive your synagogue or church affiliation if that is something that might give your family comfort during this time.

If your family is unaffiliated religiously, a spiritual or community group that feels similarly to you might be worth looking into. It's important for everyone, children and adults alike, to have the support of a community during such difficult days.

Why do people have to die, anyway?

Explain to your child that everything living is born and then dies: Dying is a natural part of living.

Plants grow and then die; animals live and then die; and people live and eventually die. As the Bible says, "To everything there is a season."

Comfort your children with the thought that most people die when they get to be really, really old.

There are several excellent books on death and dying geared to children of all different ages. The best of these are listed at the end of this book.

When your child asks this question, he isn't really asking a metaphysical question anyway. What he really wants to know is why people *he* knows and is close to have to die, and whether anyone he knows and loves is likely to die.

Try to reassure your child that it is unlikely that anyone he knows and loves will be involved. Remind him that it is your job to keep your family safe, and that you will do that.

What does dying feel like?

Tell your child that we can't really know that, since it hasn't happened to us, and the people who have died (use an example if you have one: "like Aunt Sophie") can't tell us.

If you wish, relate stories of what people who have almost died thought they saw: Lights, a tunnel, loved family members coming to greet them. If you practice a religion that has a perspective on death, this might be a good time to introduce that.

Gloss over the details of the pandemic's horror with a younger child and, if asked, say that death usually happens quickly and peacefully.

Remember that younger children often don't understand a lot of what they are hearing on the news anyway. This can either make them more or less fearful and upset, depending on what they think has happened.

(My then-5-year-old, for example, hearing that something had burned down, happily told me that he was glad the fire had burned down, "because if it had burned up, someone might have gotten hurt!")

If you hear a happy misinterpretation of this sort, and there's no older child to set them straight, it might be best to let well enough alone.

In any case, when asked about death, explain that people who die usually look relaxed and peaceful, and don't seem to be in pain.

Why did this happen?

This is one of the hardest questions to answer, because it means, to some extent, the end of your child's innocence.

Children are born trusting the world. In the aftermath of something like a pandemic, when your child asks why, you will have to convey to her that the world isn't always a safe place.

Tell your child that sometimes bad things happen and we don't always know why. Stress that usually things go well—you don't want her to feel more scared than she has to. But explain that every so often, something goes badly.

If your child is old enough to know any history, you might take this opportunity to talk about other situations in the past. The underlying message is that sometimes, there are bad things.

The important thing is to make sure the child understands that most people are good and behave nicely to each other, and that mostly the world is an ok place.

Children would much rather feel guilty than powerless, as long as they can maintain some sense of control over a situation. Thus, they may at some level feel like the situation is their fault. Be sure they understand it is no one's fault.

Will it happen here?

When your child asks if the pandemic will happen here, he wants to know if he'll be safe, and if your family will be safe.

Strangers are too distant a concept for him to worry about: He's concerned about his own family and friends.

Remind your child that until now, nothing bad has ever happened where you live, if that's true. Tell your child that in general, such terrible things hardly ever happen.

Try something like, "For hundreds of years, we've been safe living here."

Children don't really appreciate the unlikelihood of such an event occurring, but the reassurance in your voice when you say this will be helpful to them anyway.

And if you couch it in more personal terms that is still better:

"Grandma and Grandpa grew up here and nothing bad happened here; I grew up here and nothing bad happened; and I don't think anything bad will happen here."

Keep reminding your child that it is your job, as a parent, to make sure they stay safe. "Mommy and Daddy will do everything we have to keep us all safe and happy."

Did this happen because I was bad?

Children often feel guilty about events that have nothing to do with them. After a parent's divorce, they may feel their sibling fighting was responsible; after the death of a loved one they may feel it was because of the time they said they hated him.

Perhaps because children are scolded by parents frequently, when a traumatic event occurs, they may feel it was somehow their responsibility or fault for not behaving better.

What a child least wants to feel is powerless. Children want to feel that they are in control of a situation. If the choice comes down to feeling guilty (because somehow their bad behavior caused the situation) or feeling powerless, children will almost always opt for guilt.

So although your child wants to hear the reassurance that he had nothing to do with this, he is simultaneously hoping it was his fault, so that he was somehow in control of the situation.

Try explaining to your child: "Sometimes bad things happen, but it's not your fault." And then empower him in other ways—by giving him more control over his environment, or more choices that are usually not open to him, to alleviate his feelings of powerlessness.

Can I stay home from school?

During a pandemic, depending on where you live, your child may be required to stay home from school.

If you're in a location where the schools are open, but your child says he doesn't want to go to school, or claims a headache or sore throat, ask directly if he is afraid because of what happened.

If your child is distressed, keep him home for the day or part of the day. Ask if it would help if you drove him to school, or picked him up at the end. For teenagers it might be more helpful to be in school where they can process the situation with their peers.

Separation anxiety during a pandemic is a natural and common response. The younger the child, the more likely he is to express this. Parents may see clingy behavior, resistance to babysitters, and unwillingness to leave the house.

Trauma can temporarily destroy a child's previous feelings of safety; by refusing to separate, she is able to rely on the physical presence of her trusted family. Be sensitive to it, and don't push.

Occasionally, an extremely upset child may be reluctant to venture outside the house at all. On the one hand, this phobia helps the child feel more in control of the situation, because she can avoid being exposed to further trauma in what has become, to her, a scary world.

On the other hand, even this extreme reaction will not relieve her fear.

Staying at home to avoid further trauma is ultimately unsuccessful, since even inside the house a traumatized child will feel helpless and terrified, be it during the day or in nightmares.

If this problem continues, seek professional counseling for your child.

What about social distancing?

There is a whole set of new vocabulary that goes along with a pandemic, including the phrase "social distancing."

Whether or not your children ask you about social distancing explicitly, sit them down and explain it.

Tell your children that in order to keep as many people as safe as possible, especially older people who are at greater risk, you'll need to cut back on or stop going to school and other places (restaurants, shopping malls, etc.)

You'll need to cut out playdates (though you can have "virtual" playdates.) And birthday parties and big celebrations will have to be postponed until afterwards. Be sure to assure kids that you can still have fun and treats, just inside and smaller.

Is it ok to cry?

Most children won't ask this directly. Some children, in fact, evince worry by denying their fear, and loudly proclaiming their bravery.

These children are often the ones who, in the privacy of their bedrooms at night, experience terrific nightmares. The more vehement they are about their power, the more aggressive they are in their play, the more likely they are to experience an underlying fearfulness.

From children around the age of eight, especially, you may hear this question about crying guised in the form of doubt or scorn for someone who has exhibited the behavior:

"Davey was a crybaby when he heard the radio today," a friend's 7-year-old related to his father.

What he is really asking is permission to express this feeling himself, and assurance that it is an acceptable way to deal with the situation.

Give the assurance. "Crying is ok. That doesn't mean that Davey is a coward. Brave people cry when they're sad. I cried yesterday when I heard the news about what's happening in Italy. Sometimes crying can help make you feel better."

Is it ok to laugh and smile?

In the same way that some children won't be able to cry without permission, others won't be able to enjoy themselves.

Survivor guilt is a very powerful emotion, and even very young children may feel it.

Tell your child: "It seems like the whole world is so sad right now, and you may feel funny if you find yourself laughing and having a good time as if nothing happened. But you shouldn't feel bad about it. People are resilient, and that's what makes us people."

You may also find that both you and your child go through moments of denial, where you temporarily forget the entire situation. When you catch yourself engaging happily in normal activity, you may feel guilt.

You shouldn't. This intermittent denial is healthy, and encourages healing.

Persuade your child to go on with his life, as much as is possible. Play games, read books, spend time together happily as a family.

Don't make the mistake of censuring a child who is having fun, even if it is in the midst of the news coverage. You can't regulate sadness, and shouldn't.

Will there be enough food?

Many children, having heard panicked adults talking nervously about stockpiling groceries, medications, and toilet paper, may worry that there won't be enough for them to eat.

Reassure them that your family has enough food supplies to get you through, and that the supplies include treats for them, as well. Show them your assortment of food, so they see you're prepared.

It's difficult, but try as much as possible to avoid those panicked food conversations while your children are listening. It's one additional stressor that they (and you!) don't need.

What can we do to make a difference?

Even young children may ask you if there isn't something that they can do to help. People of all ages want to feel that they can make a difference, and do something helpful.

And of course they can, and doing it is guaranteed to make them feel better.

Younger children can write letters to people in the hospitals, locally or in other locales. They can draw a picture to mail to the families.

You can all light a candle together, and say a prayer if that is your inclination. You and your children can attend a virtual online prayer service or a memorial service.

Older children can join you in donating to a blood drive, or canvassing the neighbors online to raise funds for families in need.

Taking positive action will counteract feelings of helplessness and promote faster healing. Doing something helpful is empowering, and wonderfully helpful.

Why am I having bad dreams?

Children often react to situations by shutting it out of their mind as much as they can. Particularly in the event of multiple traumatic events over an extended period of time, children may find it easier to block the events from their waking hours.

It's a coping mechanism: Having dreams is the way we digest and process our life experiences. But the trauma will surface in phobias, nightmares, or other undesirable symptoms or behaviors.

There's no wonder cure for bringing your child's fears out into the open to protect her from nightmares other than processing her emotions during waking hours.

If your child complains of nightmares, try explaining it this way:

"Sometimes you have bad dreams when you've seen something scary or sad, and we're all stressed about it, even if you decide to never think about it again. If there's something that's scaring you, we can talk about it. Talking about it might help to make the bad dreams go away. It may take a while."

You might try planning with your child what he should dream; sometimes discussing what the content of his dreams could be will help. Or you might try physically chasing the tigers out from under the bed, or throwing the bad dreams out the open window.

Recognize that, during a pandemic, it may take time till the nightmares lessen. And particularly when the situation is ongoing, your child may continue to experience nightmares for a while.

Why do I keep thinking about it?

Following any traumatic incident, children frequently experience undesired, usually visual, memories of the event: Fragments flying, people screaming, hospital beds, people in scary masks and hazmat suits, enter as random images at random times.

The intrusion of such imagery is incredibly traumatic and insistent, and your child may experience panic. Certainly it is difficult for many children to banish these visual images, and very hard to stop thinking about the situation.

Tell your child that the more you talk about the event together, the less he'll think about it when he's not with you.

Over time, the memories of the event will begin to fade, and eventually he won't have to think about it much at all.

Will I ever feel normal again?

During a pandemic, children, like adults, are on an emotional rollercoaster. Some moments everything feels fine and back to normal; other moments you feel depressed and lethargic. The fact that everyone in the world is going through similar feelings doesn't make it that much better. Explain to your child that it will be like this for a while. Tell her that you, too, feel these emotional swings. Eventually, everything will feel normal again.

Don't expect your child to snap back to normal quickly. Be patient. There's a lot of processing that needs to happen to assimilate the reality of such an event.

Be prepared to listen to your child talk—or play—this through again, and again, and yet again. Much as they are frightened, children may want to reenact the incident constantly, as a way of bracing themselves emotionally for a possible return of the situation. Let them.

In the meantime, do something. Go jogging together, slap finger paint around, play a game with a lot of shouting. Try to discharge some of the excess energy.

Writing, Drawing, and Playing as Therapy

Writing, drawing, and playing can all aid children in working through some of the angst of trauma. Children often engage in these activities as a way of working through distress or other emotions that they have encountered in everyday life. A child whose mother has yelled at her because she threw cereal all over the floor might scold her doll in a similar manner, as a way of relieving her bad feelings about the scolding.

During a pandemic situation, as with any trauma, children's enactments of the situation may seem almost too detailed and intense. The very repetition is healing to the child who would otherwise consciously repress the memories of the scary events.

Children may want you to be involved in their play, as occasionally it is too frightening for them to reenact the trauma without you close by. Or they may want the freedom to emote without fear of censure or judgment that playing in privacy affords. Either way, respect their playing, and encourage it.

If the play seems monotonously similar, rather than free-spirited and versatile, it may be the post-traumatic play of a child obsessed with an incident. If the obsessive play incorporates a behavior that is different from your child's normal behavior, seek professional help for your child.

Finally, consider encouraging your child to play, write, or draw with other children who were similarly affected by the events, even if this needs to occur online. Group situations can be extremely useful in helping children work through some of their anxieties.

Writing

Suggest your child keep a journal of the ongoing event, or write a letter to one of the families affected. Or write poems, or stories, with the following themes:

- Write about your most scary nightmare
- Write how you felt when you first heard the news
- Write how you feel about it now that it's getting less scary
- Write what your life is like now
- Write what people have been saying

You can also simply encourage your child to keep a journal or diary without making suggestions. They may find an open-ended writing process particularly helpful.

Drawing

Get out the art supplies. Sit down with your child, and both of you draw. Don't make suggestions, just draw. Let your child lead, and you follow. Don't do anything too directed. If you feel you must say something, try the following:

- Draw what you feel like right now
- Paint the color you feel
- Draw your life

Or draw or paint squiggles on a piece of paper and let your child turn them into pictures. Then ask them questions about their pictures, and see what they say. Remember, the goal in play therapy is to be as non-directive as possible; you can't regulate the conversation.

Playing

Use puppets or dolls with your child. Or use dress-up clothing.

Again, remember that the goal is not to direct the play so as to "discuss" the events; the goal is to let your child play and see if she is working through the events.

Join in her play and see what she is focusing on. Although you shouldn't direct the play, you can try offering solutions or alternative endings to her play.

Children's play can be as unsettling for the adults around them as children's anger. You may feel uncomfortable watching your child play, either because of the intensity of the play or because of the content. Try not to judge, and try not to let your child see your discomfort.

For Further Reading

There are hundreds of books for adults on how children grieve and experience trauma. The most accessible of the trauma books is Lenore Terr's *Too Scared to Cry: How Trauma Affects Children – and Ultimately Us All*.

Two good adult books on how children grieve are these:
  Explaining Death to Children by Earl Grollman
  On Death and Dying by Elisabeth Kübler-Ross

A good book for adults on dealing with life's difficult questions is:
  When Bad Things Happen to Good People by Harold Kushner

Unfortunately, there are really no great books on pandemics written for children. There are many good books on grieving, however, which are worthwhile; here is just a smattering of what is available.

Books for 3-8 year olds:
When Dinosaurs Die by Laurie and Marc Brown
The Dead Bird by Margaret Brown
Nana Upstairs and Nana Downstairs by Tomie dePaoloa
Lifetimes by Bryan Mellonie and Robert Ingpen

Books for 8-12 year olds:
Little Women by Louisa May Alcott
The Big Wave by Pearl Buck
Meet the Austins by Madeleine L'Engle

Books for Teenagers:
A Death in the Family by James Agee
Green Memories by Lewis Mumford
Love Story by Erich Segal

About the Author

Fern Reiss witnessed firsthand the effects of trauma on children in Israel, Africa, and Asia. She is an honors graduate from Harvard University, and writes frequently about parenting and psychology for major magazines, including Sesame Street, Scholastic Parent and Child, Moment, and Parade. She is the first self-published writer inducted into the American Society of Journalists and Authors and was a 2005 finalist for Inc. Magazine's Entrepreneur of the Year award. Fern's other books include:

The Family Guide to Quarantine

The Publishing Game: Find an Agent in 30 Days,
The Publishing Game: Publish a Book in 30 Days, and
The Publishing Game: Bestseller in 30 Days
(all Writer's Digest Book Club selections)

The Infertility Diet: Get Pregnant and Prevent Miscarriage
(an Independent Book Publishers Association
Benjamin Franklin award winner)

Terrorism and Kids: Comforting Your Child
(an American Booksellers Association Booksense 76
winner)

The Breast Cancer Checklist

Fern runs the Expertizing "*Strategize, Publicize, Monetize*" online course for small businesses at:
```
Courses.Expertizing.com
```

She and her family live in Boston.

My Notes

How to Order This Book

If you're interested in quantity orders for your school, church, synagogue, or other organization, please contact us:

>Peanut Butter and Jelly Press
>P.O. Box 590239
>Newton, MA 02459-0002
>(617)630-0945
>info@PeanutButterAndJellyPress.com

www.ingramcontent.com/pod-product-compliance
Lightning Source LLC
LaVergne TN
LVHW041336080426
835512LV00006B/489